FRONT COVER PHOTO:
A barn shot during a rare snow
storm outside the city of Pine
Bluff in South Central Arkansas.

BACK COVER PHOTO:
An old barn with rough hewn
plank siding, has part of its tin
roof held down by old tires.

DEDICATION

This book is dedicated to the PBCDF Project-Pine Bluff Arsenal
and Parsons Corporation who brought me to Arkansas. Also, to
my wife Gira, my daughter Seema, my son Sameer, my brothers
Visubhai and Kantibhai, my nephews Ashok, Sunil and Atul,
my neices Manda and Devi, and the rest of my Sima family.
And also to Barney Sellers, noted for his colorful Ozark and
southern rural scenes who inspired me
in my photographic endeavors.

In Memory of
my Grandparents and Parents.

SPECIAL THANKS...

to Ted Owens of Bearden and all the wonderful people
I met while traveling the back roads of Arkansas and
for their kind permission
to allow me to photograph their barns and buildings.
Without their kindness and help,
this book would not have been possible.
Also, my grateful thanks to Bedford's Camera their
help in scanning these photo for reproduction,
and their excellent photo seminars.

D1208559

Book designed by David R. Greene and Naran Patel.
Other publication team members: Scott Hunter, Billy Trent and Coleen Schroder.
© Copyright 2004 by Naran Patel. All rights reserved.
Library of Congress Control Number: 2004096173 ISBN Number: 0976051672
No part of this book may be reprinted in any form, including electronic or mechanical means, such as information
storage without written permission from Naran Patel.
Book manufactured in Korea

All the photographs in this book are available as custom printed images. Autographed, personalized copies of this book and all photos by Naran Patel are available as well.
To order contact the author direct:
Naran Patel, 7882 Sunflower Lane, La Palma, California, 90623. E-mail:naranhallmark@aol.com

About the Author

Naran Patel was born in an agricultural community in India, where he grew up working in his father's fields of cotton, rice, wheat, and other crops. He was young, but can remember working in those fields by hand, without the aid of all of the mechanical equipment available today.

At an early age, he moved to America. Growing up in Los Angeles, California, he truly missed the beauty of the rural life that he experienced as a youngster. However, he was able to capture so much life in the photographs that he took throughout the country, as the profession (engineering and construction) he chose after leaving college, enhanced his travels all over the United States and foreign countries.

With both a chemical and mechanical engineering degree, Naran interfaces the construction and start up of plants, recently designed specifically for disarming both chemical and explosive weapons. He received his B.S. in mechanical engineering from California State University in Los Angeles, and an M.S. in chemical engineering from the University of Southern California (USC). After completing his education, he returned to India to marry. He soon returned to the United States, where his career took off, and he had the luxury of being in a position to utilize his photography at social events, holiday celebrations, weddings, and local festivals. And so his reputation began to grow as a photographer. It became more than just a hobby, his pictures now tell a story.

After locating to Arkansas, Naran's thirst for the outdoors emerged with more enthusiasm because there were so many interesting subjects to capture in pictures. The strong roots and memories of the rural culture that he so loved was nurtured once more.

For the past four years, Naran has been separated from his family and friends who remain in California, while he oversees construction of a Plant in Pine Bluff, Arkansas; one of a handful of sites in the U.S. that stores chemical weapons scheduled for destruction. However, as you will soon see in the following pages, Naran will leave a legacy of memorable events and romanticism in his quest for that perfectly captured photo. He and his family will be proud that he spent so much painstaking time in collecting a history from all over the world to enjoy for years to come. His pride shows through in his work, his family, and his hobby. Life promotes his hobby, photography, on a grand scale as you will see.

Naran's photographs illustrate his enthusiasm for his hobby, his artistic abilities in how he captures the life, nature, wildlife, and so much more, and the energy with which he approaches a scene. He passes time on the weekends traveling throughout Arkansas. He has accumulated thousands of remarkable photos that have been carefully laid out and labeled in a huge set of albums. Within these pages, are a selection of barns carefully chosen from his albums.

Naran's beautiful photography takes you through the back roads and out of the way places to show you a cross section of barns from modern to pre-statehood. As you wander through the pages, you will be treated to a visual feast of rural life in Arkansas. So sit back, relax, and slowly turn the pages of this outstanding display of photographs that take you through a brilliant and talented journey of a rural country boy, a true American at heart. You will want to revisit these pages again and again.

Barns of Arkansas
A photo journal by Naran Patel

As man moved away from his hunter/gatherer way of life and began to cultivate crops, domesticate animals, and create permanent dwellings, a problem developed, how to provide meat for his table, and hides for clothing and leather goods. Over time the domestication of animals solved this problem.

Undoubtedly, the first innovation was probably a fenced inclosure to both protect them from predators and keep them from wandering too far. In warmer climates this would have been an adequate solution, but as man spread over the less temperate areas of the earth, a more substantial means of protecting his domesticated stock had to be found.

The first such buildings may have been little more than a lean-to within the fenced corral. As farming became more sophisticated, the creation of a separate building for livestock and farming equipment was developed and barns became a distinctive fixture in rural life. As the New World began to be colonized by Europeans each group brought with them distinctive styles of barns that were common to their individual country.

Arkansas has a great many barns throughout the state, but as cities expand and housing developments gobble up farm land, old barns are fast disappearing. Naran Patel has spent the past three years documenting these wonderful buildings with his camera. Some of these barns are new and in use as are some that are very old. There is a great variety of styles and building techniques shown in these pages. We hope you enjoy this pictorial tour of barns in rural Arkansas.

This double wing barn with a distinctive silhouette of an Angus bull painted on the roof was photographed on a cattle ranch in northern Arkansas. The exterior corral fence is constructed of sturdy steel tubing.

A closer view of the same barn showing the breeze way running through the center of the building. The front and rear outside walls of the main structure are covered with lap siding, while the wings on either side have vertical siding. The loft windows may have once contained glass panes, now long gone.

Inset: A curious dog and bull check each other out.

This is a typical chicken house (barn) distinguished by its open sides and low sloping roof. In northwest Arkansas they have replaced many traditional barns as farmers switched from conventional farms to chicken ranches. The common construction of these houses involves a wood frame w corrugated metal roofs and ends. The sides are open to allow cross ventilation during warm weather. To keep the chickens from escaping, chicken wire attached across the openings. Fans are installed inside to produce air circulation during hot weather, and heaters keep the building warm during winter.

A view of the open side of the barn with curious chickens inspecting the photographer. This view shows the chicken wire mentioned on the previous page.

This is a three story double wing barn. The wings had several possible uses. Farm equipment was often stored here as well as wagons, buggies and tack. Some were divided into horse or cattle stalls. The extension of the peak over the loft helps block wind and rain from entering.

An old barn that has seen better days, although it is still in use. The original shingled roof was replaced long ago by corrugated tin. An add on lean-to can be seen in the right side of the picture.

An interior shot of an old barn showing the hand hewn beams and an old buckboard wagon. Note the loose rock foundation holding up the inside room walls. The room next to the wagon may have been a harness or tack room. Like many old barns, the floor was dirt.

A close up shot of the carpentry work showing the dovetail joined hand hewn logs.
Sometimes the builder used green logs when making mortise and tenon joints.
As the timbers dried out, they would swell and make a tight joint.

A typical barn with an add on lean-to for equipment storage. The main building sits on a mortared native stone foundation. Before the advent of hay rolls, farmers would store green hay in the loft of their barns to dry out. Because as the green hay dries it produces a great deal of heat, most lofts were well ventilated to cool down the drying hay.

This is a rounded roof barn with an add on lean-to. Before sheet metal roofing, covering this roof with shingles must have been quite a chore. The vertical siding allows the circulation of air through the inside of the barn. Unfortunately the beautiful weathered wood has made old barns vulnerable to people looking for unique and attractive den walls.

This old barn while in sad shape is still recognizable as a double wing structure with hand hewn planks and timbers. The doors on the loft entrance and the first floor opening have long disappeared. On the right side of the ground floor entrance you can just make out the dovetailed timbers that make up the interior walls.

Horses walk toward the photographer in a pasture beside a white washed horse barn with a tin roof. Open side stalls run the length of the ground floor.

An old double wing barn stands in the background replaced by a livestock barn in the foreground and an equipment shed behind it. The modern method of rolling hay has made lofts for drying hay and hay bailers obsolete. A lone cow checked out the photographer as he made this shot.

Inset: This is a close up shot of the corral gate with it's many hinges that stands just to the left of the cow.

Surrounded by a hog wire fence this old barn is open at the front from the ground to the peak of the roof. While it is in poor shape, it is still in use. The vertical supports appear to be rough cut logs like the fence posts in the foreground.

A single wing barn is framed by the doorway of a shed. Rolls of hay can be seen drying in the first floor doorway.

Some farmers sold space for advertising on the roof of their barns like this one depicted here. The copy on the right reads "neck, back, joint, pain". On the left is a map guiding you to the office in Sheridan. The barn is a double wing style with horizontal siding.

This barn is an unusual version of a double wing barn with its squared off front, vented roof, and cupula. The sign above the door reads, "Morton's Salt". This is another example of barn advertising.

A modern white double wing barn with a tin roof and white plank fence corral, sits just beyond a ripe cotton field.

A cat stands on the fence and looks toward the barn,perhaps contemplating a meal of field mice which often infest barns. Many an unwary city child has tried to pick up a barn kitten with disastrous results. Most barn cats are wild and will scratch and bite if cornered. The farmers tolerate them to keep the rodent population in check.

This old single wing barn sits on a slight slope. Except for the front, the wood siding has been sheathed over with tin. The shingled roof has been replaced with corrugated iron. Behind the barn can be seen a round silo for grain storage.

This old single wing barn has an add on lean-to on the right side. The vertical wood siding appears in fairly good shape for the building's obvious age. The sign nailed to the left side of the front reads: "Posted NO Trespassing".

The long low sloping roof and corral suggest that this is a dairy or
horse barn. Both the roof and sides are sheathed in tin.

A tall silo sits behind a double winged barn with a tin roof and vertical plank siding. The wing
in view has four openings to park wagons, buggies and farm equipment out of the weather.

This photo paints a sad picture. The barn is near collapse. Its side walls are giving way to dry rot and its interior frame has all but fallen in. Weeds choke its corral and the fence is rotting away.

This abandoned cotton gin, stands in mute testimony to a time when cotton was king in Arkansas. The long dock allowed wagons to load bales from the gin. The raw cotton was off loaded from wagons and ginned and bailed inside.

A windmill used to pump well water stands beside a double wing barn. The left wing facing the barn is open to allow equipment to be sheltered from the rain. The sign on the door at the front of the barn says: "Posted No Trespassing". The windmill is no longer working.

Another view of the barn from the previous page
shows an outbuilding and silo behind the barn.

The outside walls as well as the doors of this old barn are made of round logs. Two side wings cover farm equipment. Notice the three white bird houses on the front of the barn.

Inset: An outbuilding to the front and left of the barn and out of the picture, has a collapsed roof and missing siding, yet there is another bird house attached to the wall just above the door.

Another view of the barn from the previous page shows three iron gates to keep the cattle out, or in.

An early morning mist gives this barn a ghostly look as though it is fading away before your very eyes.This may be a prophetic photo as more old barns succumb to neglect, high winds, and ice storms. *Inset:* Bright red orange fall leaves contrast the grey weathered barn boards.

This double wing barn is in surprisingly good shape for its age. A part of the roof has been patched with asphalt shingles. A typical barn of this vintage would have had stalls for milking cows, as well as stalls for horses or mules. In addition there would have been a tack room with tools for repairing leather harness. Bins for grain to feed the livestock usually were placed at one end of the ground floor.

A shot of a pretty single wing modern barn.

In the distance stands a modern barn with vertical steel siding and two open wings on either side.

Inset: A donkey stands in front of the white door of the barn as though waiting to be let in..

Another shot of the barn showing the farm equipment under the open
left wing.Under the right wing can be seen hay rolls.

Inset: An antique buckboard wagon is stored
within the barn. These wagons were the
pickup truck of the horse and buggy days.

An pole barn with a sheet metal roof has open sides for easy access to equipment.

Inset: A closeup shot of hay rolls stored out of the rain.

Another view of the pole barn with the farm equipment
parked under the overhang.

Inset: A closeup shot of some
of the stored machinery.

A single wing barn with an extended lean-to is home to a herd of Brahma cattle. Notice the herringbone siding on the front of the barn.

Inset: A Brahma cow watches as her calf has an early breakfast.

As Naran prepared to snap another shot, the resident cattle gathered together for a group photo.

This old barn fell victim to a winter ice storm. In its weakened state, it could not bear up under the crushing weight of the ice.

An unusual double wing cattle barn with vented roof and sides.

Inset: A Jersey cow patiently feeds her calf.

Although it is still in use, this barn seems to be coming apart at he seams. The front, roof and side walls are separating. The door has come off its track, but the farmer is confident enough to park his tractor inside. Notice the cattle pens across the road from the barn.

This view of the barn from the previous page shows
six small silos in a row.

The rotting red siding has been replaced in several places on this barn. An open lean-to on the right side protects farm equipment.

Inset: A hay bailer sits under the over hang. This piece of equipment is fast becoming obsolete with the advent of hay rolls.

Snow blankets two barns and hay rolls on a frosty winter morning

Cows cluster together on this cold snowy day and stare at Naran as
if questioning why anyone would be out in such miserable weather.

This barn has become a storage building. Daylight can be seen shining
through the cracks in the horizontal siding.

Inset: This close up of the door way shows
a large stack of old barn lumber.

An interior shot of a barn showing a milking stall. Against the wall is a feed trough. The farmer would place hay in the trough. When the cow stuck its head through the horizontal slats the farmer would slip another slat or rope across above the cow's neck so she could not back out until the milking was finished.

This stall door is held shut by a sliding wood slat. In the far upper left corner of the photo, you can see that the top rail is almost chewed into. Probably caused by a nervous or bored horse. Horses have upper and lower front teeth, while cows have only lower front teeth.

The owner of this barn no longer uses it for its original purpose.
It now holds a variety of wood and other things that some would
call junk.

Behind the barn from the previous page, is an old outbuilding that the owner uses for a work shop. Lying scattered around the exterior are piles of raw materials to be used for future projects.

Inside the shop there is hardly a bare spot in the floor or walls.
Tools, material, and equipment are scattered everywhere.

Cans and tools cover most of the work bench in the shop. Old hand tools still in use, hang on the wall above the bench. Under the bench are more tools and materials. In spite of all this seeming chaos, many a fine and beautifully crafted piece of wood work has been produced here,

This is another wall with more antique tools. Handsaws sit in a rack while drawknives, gouges, and a handmade bowsaw hang from pegs on the wall. On the bench can be seen wood drills, a can of paint brushes, punches, and chisels.

An old dinner bell is mounted on a post in the foreground. Behind the bell stands an old horse barn with a tack room on its right. Bells like this on were used to call the field hands in for dinner.

A closer look at the barn shows the vertical siding and steel livestock gate at the front of the left wing of the barn.

Inset: An old frying pan hangs by a rusty nail on the wall of the tack room.

Long abandoned, this log barn sits surrounded by trees. It was not uncommon for farmers clearing land for farming to use the logs from the trees they cut as building material. The logs on this barn were stripped of their bark, dried and notched at the ends for assembly.

Another view of the log barn shows the notched interlocking corners of the log construction.
Upon closer examination, the barn appears to sit directly on the ground without a rock or
cement foundation, which was not uncommon in earlier days.

From the inside you can see the gaps in the log walls.
This barn was possibly used to hold livestock.

The loft area shows the tin roof and rafters that may have
been replaced sometime in the past with milled lumber.

This barn with its herringbone siding sits in the lowest spot in the field. A ramp leads up to the barn doors. The floor is wood.

The other end of the barn is level with the ground outside.
A concrete foundation supports the outer walls.

Under the barn you can see support columns and pillars. This arrangement may keep the barn from flooding during rainy weather.

This is an unusual barn door hinge made of horse shoes and nailed to the barn
with, of course, horse shoe nails. In the following few pages we will show you
some interesting clutter that you find around barns.

The photo on the left is a barn wall still life. Whether done intentionally or not it makes an interesting arrangement with its indian corn, horseshoes, and plow blade. The photo on the right with chains,wheels, and old license plate might bring a high price at an art auction in New York.

A bucket hangs from a well pump still in use. Before electricity, almost all farms had one. The lucky ones had a smaller version attached to the sink in the farm house. In the right photo a mower blade stands upright like a medieval torture device waiting for its next victim.

An old well bucket hangs by a chain and pulley in front of an abandoned farm house. The photo at right shows an old barn door and through the cracks you can see a barn that has collapsed, a victim of an ice storm.

This rural mail box is made from an old plow. Plows like this were used throughout America until replaced by the tractor. This is a practical use for a piece of equipment no longer needed for the purpose it was intended.

This mail box sits on an old treadle sewing machine base that became obsolete when electricity came to rural Arkansas.

This old barn with its broad plank siding and tin roof has seen
better days. Today it serves as a livestock barn.

Along the side of the barn is a crib where the livestock are fed. The narrow slats allow the cattle or horses to stick just their noses through to get the hay and thus restricting the amount of hay they can pull from the crib,assuring that all the cattle will be fed.

A log chicken house may be over kill but the chickens don't seem to
care. At one time it might have been a smoke house .

A Plymouth Rock rooster and his hens, pose for the photographer.

This small double wing barn had rough cut, un-painted
siding and corrugated tin roof.

As Naran was reloading his camera for a different view of the barn a curious steer approaches to check him out.

...and he brought his friends.

This ramshackle old barn contrasts the brilliant fall leaves of the tree behind it.

This double wing barn almost seems to shiver on a cold winter morning. Patches of snow can be seen in the pasture.

The roof overhang on this log smoke house
is almost as long as the building itself.

When Naran went to the the back of the barn he found that it had
some help standing up.

Another old log smoke house that seems to need some help standing. A paneled door swings on wrought iron hinges.

This outbuilding is made of striped bark logs. The wing was probably added on long after the original structure was built. Notice the shingle siding on the add-on.

This old barn with its vertical siding and a door leaning against the opening is protected bay a huge old oak tree.

Another old log building that was also once a smoke house sits
far enough from the other farm buildings to not be a fire hazard.

Snow blankets a log barn and out building.
Some of the out building's roof is missing.

About the only thing left that show this barns original construction, is
the right corner of the walls with its dovetail mortise log walls.

Two old trucks sit in front of an old barn that is unusual because
the breezeway runs crossways to the roofline.

Cattle stand in a snowy field outside an old barn
used as a livestock shelter.

This maybe the smallest barn in the state. It sits in the middle of a snowy field on a bleak winter morning.

This low slung barn was possibly made from available native trees cut to clear the land. The horizontal siding appears to be rough cut.

Two barns are framed by large trees. The left one was shot on an early winter morning, while the other barn was shot on a bright spring day.

A wagon sits under the lean-to of an old barn with vertical siding.
The undergrowth indicates that the wagon has been there
for some time.

Although this barn has no paint except for a panel over the loft window, it seems to be in pretty good condition. It is currently used as a cattle barn.

A closer look at the front of the barn shows two buggy wheels hung on either side of the loft opening. A metal gate blocks the doorway to keep livestock in, or out.

This old double wing barn sits abandoned on a homestead overgrown with weeds. Another barn can be seen through the breezeway. The barn doors are missing, as well as the loft door.

An old barn and outbuilding can be seen behind a board fence enclosure. The building in the foreground has an extended lean-to side with an added half wall running across the front.

Another view of the outbuilding in the foreground of the previous picture shows the concrete post foundation and double doors in the front. The cracks between the vertical are covered by narrow furring strips.

This old barn looks so fragile that it might fall over if you
breathed too hard on it. Notice the trees that have grown up in
front of the door.

At one time this barn had wood siding that is now sheathed in corrugated metal roofing. Is is currently used as an equipment shed.

A guard dog eyed Naran from behind a chain link fence when he took this picture of a double wing barn that has seen better days. Looking at the interior, it appears that the loft floor is completely gone. Corrugated tin keeps out the weather on the first floor.

An old log smoke house has partially collapsed on its right side and some of the roof on that side is missing. Once again you can see the dovetail joints that lock the logs together at the corners of the building.

Still in use, this stock barn sits inside a gated pasture. Some repair
has been made to its front wall.

A closer look at the barn from the previous page shows the patch job and a sheath of corrugated tin around the lower portion of the left wall.

It is hard to imagine that this barn is still in use. The front support for the roof of the left wing is missing and some of the corrugated metal roof is missing.

A three story barn, silo, windmill, and out building were
photographed on an early winter morning.

Cattle feed on a roll of hay in a pasture in front of a low-slung
hay barn filled to the rafters with hay rolls.

A closer look at the cattle as they feed, ignoring the photographer.

This log building is in such sad shape it's hard to tell for sure what its original purpose was.

Inset: At one time someone may have lived here.
Notice the old 33 ⅓ records in the doorway.

This little barn is on the verge of collapse. Although the wind and weather have played havoc with its shingled roof, quite a few still cling to it.

Farm animals don't get many visitors, that must be why they always approached Naran as he tried to set up to photograph barns where the livestock could see him.

This beautiful red barn with white trim, sits
at the edge of a freshly mowed pasture.

The fields in front of this old barn are sprinkled with a light snow. The double wings and vertical siding is a typical barn pattern in Arkansas. The grey unpainted siding on the the barn walls only seems to emphasize a cold winter day.

This scene would look good on a Christmas card cover.

Naran shot this picture during a rare snow storm just outside Pine
Bluff in south central Arkansas.

Snow blankets these two barn roofs and rolls of hay. The outer layer of the rolls help insulate the rolls from rain and mildew. By rolling the hay tightly, the necessity of placing them in the loft is no longer necessary

Hay rolls covered with snow sit beside a barn, built on a slope. The barns
vertical siding has warped and appears to be pulling away from the frame.

An old abandoned house framed by an old fence was just too dramatic
to leave out of the book. We apologize that it isn't a barn.

A closer look at the abandoned dwelling. One can only wonder,
who lived there, and where are they now?

Most of this barn is hidden behind a wire
fence covered with vines.

Herringbone siding covers the front wall of this barn. To the right
is a low slung livestock barn.

A livestock barn peeks out from a maple tree
dressed in brilliant crimson fall color.

This a beautiful shot of an old barn nestled in a
rainbow of fall color.

A beautiful fiery red tree appears to be holding up this old barn.

This new red barn competes well with the emerging fall colors of
the surrounding trees.

An old double wing barn was once as bright as the barn on the previous page, but its brilliant red paint has faded.

Evening shadows fall on this triple story barn with its vented roof top.

Behind the hay rolls in the foreground a double
wing barn peeks out from the woods.

This barn is in better shape than the board fence in
the foreground.

Another view of the barn shows a better fence.

This is a three story barn with a vented peak, and double wings.

A smoke house sits in a field surrounded
by a wire and buggy wheel fence.

Another shot of the buggy wheels used as a fence.

Three openings in the front of this barn lead to the two wings interior. The side of both wings are open as well to facilitate the movement of farm equipment.

Believe it or not, this barn is still in use.

Undergrowth stands ready to swallow up this old double wing barn. Vines creep up the fence posts surrounding it.

Inset: A closer view of the front of the barn shows the detail of the opening and the siding.

Once again this barn is still in use, even though part of the main roof is
missing as well as the entire cover of the overhang in front of the door.

Unusual shingle siding can be seen on the front of this barn starting just above the roof line and continuing down to the ceiling of the first floor.

A smoke house sits in the middle of a field. An attached ladder
leads up to the vented roof.

This is a log barn with an open loft.

This double wing barn has settled so much that it has twisted its
horizontal siding.

A severe windstorm took away most of the front of this barn.

Snow covers the tops of the hay rolls and most of the ground. The row of windows on the side of the barn behind the hay suggest that its original use was for livestock, either a milking barn or for horses.

A log props up the corner of the added on lean-to roof. The original building was the log portion.

An old flat bed truck sits in front of an outhouse. The truck
replaced the buckboard wagon of the horse and buggy era.

Looking out from inside a barn through the cracks
in the broken barn doors.

The original doors on this barn have been replaced with
lattice panels.

The doors are missing on this old barn. They were probably removed because the barn settled.

This huge building may have been used for grain storage. Its entire surface
is sheathed in steel. Concrete pillars hold it off the ground.

A donkey stands and stares curiously at Naran in front of this magnificent double wing barn with herringbone siding.

Inset: The curious donkey turned and faced the camera for his portrait.

A double wing livestock barn with center posts running down the
middle of the main room.

A close up view of the ridge overhang protecting the loft opening.

An interior shot of the center bracing running
the length of the breezeway.

A trough runs along the side of the
breezeway for feeding livestock.

This barn could serve as a small aircraft hanger.

Maybe this building doesn't qualify as a barn but, with the farm tool collection hung all over the outer walls, we thought it should be in the book. A buckboard wagon sits under the left wing of the building.

Another view of the building showing more of the collection.
Inset: A better view of the buckboard wagon.

Single trees, double trees and horse shoes cover this side of the barn.
Inset: A better view of the wagon that shows it's in very good shape.

A closer view of the harness trappings.

A red barn beside the other building is covered with horse collars
and more tack.

Even the posts of the wings are hung with tools.

A view of both buildings from the previous pages. Through the wing of the second building in the photo you can see another structure with more things hanging on its sides.

Only the long roof of the barn peeks over the brush. Some of the
roof is missing at each end.

Rough remodeling has changed this barn. The barn doors were
removed and the opening filled in. A floor
and steps have been added..

A view showing the back of the barn with its opening filled in as well.

This double wing barn sits on a slope. The wide wings provide cover for livestock and farm equipment.

From inside the barn you can see that the loft is long gone.
Lumber is scattered throughout the inside.

An old buggy sits in a stall among the lumber
scattered around the floor.

A side view of the buggy shows that one of the back wheels is missing.

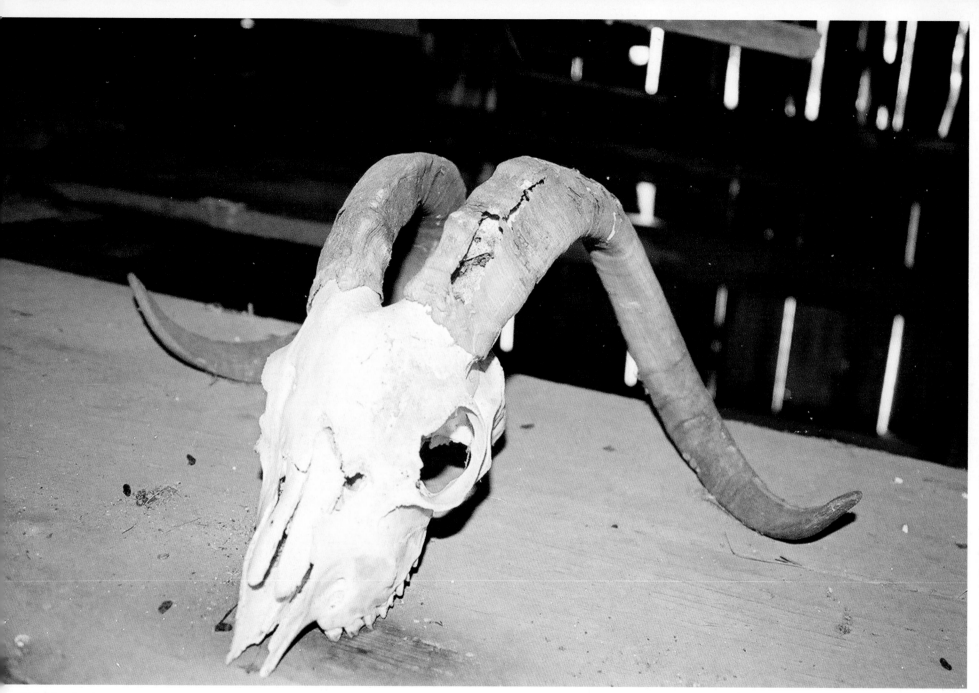

Within the barn a ram's skull rests on a shelf.

This is an unusual double wing barn with vented sides under the
top roof. Double gates block the breezeway and a half wall runs
down the right side.

This barn with vertical siding has an add on wing on the right side with a gate blocking its entrance.

This old barn with some missing siding is still in use.

A Sears medallion is still attached to this old fence. The lettering around the edge of the medallion reads "DAVID BRAIDED FENCE".

These two Gulf fuel pumps stand near a barn. Many farms had fuel storage tanks to keep the equipment running.

Acknowledgements

Since I left India in the early 60's, I took photos in all of my travels, but I was especially interested at the time in capturing people, festivals, and social events. After my schooling, as my business traveling increased, my association with some of the individuals I will mention shortly influenced my hobby. Capturing images took on a whole new meaning to me. I became very serious about collecting and organizing my photos taken all over the world. I had a renewed vigor in the way that I portrayed and displayed images that would be seen by others. The quality improved and innovative ways to capture the scene or object became paramount in my photographic effort. It is exciting and challenging to find that rare subject matter.

My photographic career has been shaped a great deal by the photographers, Barney Sellers and Tim Ernst, both from Arkansas. They are two of the leading photographers in Arkansas. I have accompanied them throughout the wilderness of this beautiful state, and down many of Arkansas's country roads. They have become my mentors.

Another person who has inspired and encouraged me to publish this book is David Greene, a North Little Rock artist. He was introduced to me by Scott hunter, who further inspired and led me into my preparation for this book. In addition, I wish to thank David Greene, who has spent so many hours selecting and organizing these pictures. Mr. Greene is a well-known artist in the Little Rock area. Without the assistance and encouragement from these two gentlemen, this project would not be at this stage. Also, my special thanks to Billy Trent for his help in scanning, color separation and finalizing the design of this book. It was a pleasure working with David, Billy and Scott.

I would like to thank the staff of the photo processing facility at Sam's Club in West Little Rock for their special attention to my specific instructions to developing my pictures. Their prompt service and quality products helped make the completion of this book possible.

Coming to Arkansas "The Natural State", meeting and learning from mentors, and my association with AOPC (Arkansas Out Door Photographers Club) of Little Rock has helped my photo hobby take on an advanced quality that I believe is illustrated in my book.

Lastly, a plea to you, the reader holding this book in your hands. The strong country tradition, along with the pride that we have in the entire state of Arkansas, is one of the most valuable traditions on earth. If we destroy these things, we destroy ourselves. By projecting these values to the world by the means of good photography, we can help preserve the history around us.

It is my hope and wish that you will gain a measure of appreciation of all that we have by viewing the unique images in this book. Take that appreciation with you, and do everything you can to celebrate, protect, and preserve our state's magnificent rural lands, country images, and continue the support of Arkansas as "The Natural State".